homecraft folkart

20 beautiful and timeless home-made gift ideas

homecraft **folkart**

20 beautiful and timeless home-made gift ideas

simona hill

southwater

This edition is published by Southwater

Southwater is an imprint of Anness Publishing Ltd
Hermes House, 88–89 Blackfriars Road, London SE1 8HA
tel. 020 7401 2077; fax 020 7633 9499; info@anness.com

© Anness Publishing Ltd 1999, 2002

Published in the USA by Southwater, Anness Publishing Inc.
27 West 20th Street, New York, NY 10011; fax 212 807 6813

This edition distributed in the UK by The Manning Partnership
251–253 London Road East, Batheaston, Bath BA1 7RL
tel. 01225 852 727; fax 01225 852 852; sales@manning-partnership.co.uk

This edition distributed in the USA by National Book Network
4720 Boston Way, Lanham, MD 20706
tel. 301 459 3366; fax 301 459 1705; www.nbnbooks.com

This edition distributed in Canada by General Publishing
895 Don Mills Road, 400–402 Park Centre, Toronto, Ontario M3C 1W3
tel. 416 445 3333; fax 416 445 5991; www.genpub.com

This edition distributed in Australia by Sandstone Publishing
Unit 1, 360 Norton Street, Leichhardt, New South Wales 2040
tel. 02 9560 7888; fax 02 9560 7488; sales@sandstonepublishing.com.au

This edition distributed in New Zealand by The Five Mile Press (NZ) Ltd
PO Box 33-1071 Takapuna, Unit 11/101-111 Diana Drive, Glenfield, Auckland 10
tel. (09) 444 4144; fax (09) 444 4518; fivemilenz@clear.net.nz

Publisher: Joanna Lorenz
Project editor: Simona Hill
Designer: Bobbie Colgate-Stone
Editorial reader: Kate Sillence

Previously published as *Folk Art Gifts*

1 3 5 7 9 10 8 6 4 2

ACKNOWLEDGEMENTS
The publishers would like to thank the following project makers: Penny Boylan for the Country Angel;
Andrew Newton-Cox for the Colonial-style Birdhouse; Tessa Evelegh for the Shaker-style Spice Wreath, Appliquéd Scented Sachets and
Heart of Wheat; Lucinda Ganderton for the Hearts and Hands Throw; Andrew Gilmore for the Wirework Hook Rack;
Melody Griffiths for the Traditional Cross-stitch Sampler; Mary Maguire for the Fluted Sconce and Twisted Heart Spice Rack;
Deborah Schneebeli Morrell for the Punched Tin Tree Decorations, Heart-carved Pumpkin and Paper-cut Eggs; and Stewart and Sally Walton
for the Patchwork Cushion Cover, Rolling Pin Holder, Painted Chequerboard, Bridal Chest, Painted Sheep Sign and Decoy Birds.

Thanks to the following photographers: Michelle Garrett, Janine Hosegood, Tim Imrie, Lizzie Orme, David Parmiter,
Debbie Patterson, Graham Rae, Heini Schneebeli, Steve Tanner, Peter Williams, Mark Wood, Polly Wreford.

Contents

INTRODUCTION   6

METALWORK   10

NEEDLEWORK   20

WOODWORK   34

NATURE'S STORE   48

TEMPLATES   60

INDEX   64

Introduction

IN ANY COMMUNITY, however isolated or impoverished, creativity will emerge. Our need to beautify our surroundings and to express our identity is irrepressible. What has come to be known as folk art is the work of ordinary men and women expressing this urge in an unsophisticated way, relying on locally available materials, the colours and shapes around them, and their natural artistic ability and ingenuity. The vitality and directness of their work gives it an immediate appeal. We recognize its domestic nature; we can relate it to our own homes and everyday tasks; we sometimes feel that we could have created the objects ourselves.

The hallmark of folk art is tradition: its styles have evolved slowly, using the same motifs, the same colours, the same materials (often recycled). It is the product of communities rather than individuals – though the work may be that of a single artist, he or she is always drawing on a shared artistic heritage.

The familiar motifs of folk art became highly stylized with constant repetition and adaptation, but all had their own symbolic significance. Some, such as the tree of life, appear in the decorative work of many cultures. Religion provided the symbolic meaning for many folk motifs: for example, the peacock stood for the Resurrection and the five-pointed star for the birth of Christ. The popularity of the tulip stemmed from the Dutch "tulip madness" of the seventeenth century. Many of the most commonly used symbols stood for love or friendship, above all the heart, which could represent both divine and earthly love.

The most vigorous folk art of the past was often produced by pioneering groups of settlers in foreign lands – such as the Pennsylvania Dutch and other European immigrants who settled on the Eastern Seaboard of North America in the seventeenth century. Having escaped from the privations and oppressions of their native homelands, they

Above: A French punched tinware cheese strainer and earthenware jugs.

Above: Patchwork and quilting offered a creative outlet to women. Right: A stylized patriotic painting of Lord and Lady Washington.

nevertheless looked back to their European roots for a sense of cultural identity, and their new colonial home acted as a melting pot into which various strands of European skills and traditions were poured. German woodcarvers, French and Italian glassmakers, Dutch painters and English weavers and quilters all took their national and local styles, motifs and conventions with them to their new home.

In the emergent colonies, a gradual homogenizing of styles took place to produce a distinctive form. Itinerant painters and decorators roamed the countryside offering specialist craft services, and in so doing took patterns, colours and techniques from one community to the next. Both the tulip, which had been so celebrated in the folk art of Holland, and the heart, beloved by the Scandinavians became widely adopted as favourite motifs. In Mexico, the artistic tradition of Central America was injected with the Moorish-influenced culture of the Spanish settlers.

The art of the people is also the product of ingenuity in the face of meagre resources. Unable to buy carpets, seafaring families cut pieces of canvas from old sails and painted them with complex geometric patterns. Immigrant communities stencilled their walls in imitation of wallpaper. When fabrics were hard to afford, they were recycled, giving rise to a rich tradition of pieced quilts. Plaited or braided rag rugs were originally made from strips of worn-out clothing, needing no equipment other than a pin to hold the end of the plait together and a needle and thread to create the coil.

This kind of decorative art centred on the home. Needlecrafts were the province of women, and girls were taught to sew from an early age. In the years before their betrothal and marriage, they created and embroidered the linen for their new household, enough to fill the traditional bridal chest they would be given as a wedding gift. A fine "friendship" quilt was a communal project made as a gift for a newly married couple. Kitchens were filled with decorated utensils, from painted salt boxes to lovingly carved spoons and punched tin lanterns.

Above: Simple painted motifs adorn the inset panels of this chest.

Above: The Amish doll is distinctive for her lack of facial features. Her clothes are scaled-down versions of those her owner would have worn.

Above: A modern salt box painted with geometric motifs.

Above: Sewing boxes were often decorated with pretty, floral patterns and often carried the owner's initials.

Very few of the artefacts that are categorized as "folk art" were made without a purpose in view: people made furniture, rugs and utensils as they needed them, and the decorative elements were a natural extension of the craftsmanship that went into the making of a functional piece. There would have been no place in a household for articles whose decoration interfered with their efficiency.

The more we are surrounded by the disposable and the mass-produced, the more we come to appreciate the appeal of artefacts made of natural materials that show signs of loving and careful use, such as wood polished by long handling, or linen that grows softer with washing: things that become more beautiful as they acquire a patina of age. Yet the artisans' creations that we collect avidly today were often considered disposable too. It was not until 1924, when a New York exhibition of American folk art brought together pieces collected by contemporary artists, that their intrinsic value began to be recognized by a wider world, and therefore by country people themselves.

Until this point folk art went undocumented and unvalued, and the traditional skills that went into its making were seriously undermined by nineteenth-century industrialization and popular clamour for the products of the new age. Even in pre-industrial days, hand-made artefacts were not necessarily considered to be worth keeping: an old patchwork quilt, for instance, might well be recycled as the filling for a new one.

These days, partly because so much has been destroyed, recycled or simply worn out, the folk art of the past has become a rare and valued commodity. *Folk Art Gifts* contains a collection of 20 projects for you to make, drawing on the rich and diverse cultural heritage of the world-wide folk art tradition. Each project, whether it is made of fabric, metal, wood or natural materials, recalls a simpler lifestyle of a bygone era. Such objects need not be confined to the past: objects of true integrity are those that are fitted to their function and are beautiful to look at, this is as true today as it was in the past.

Metalwork

METALWORKING SKILLS developed over thousands of years, and blacksmiths and other metalworkers were central figures in every traditional community, creating many of the most important and durable essentials for life, from agricultural tools and cooking pots to weapons. The decoration of metals has just as long a history as the materials themselves, demonstrating the skills of the smith and the power or value of the artefact. In the folk art tradition, decoration on metal was often functional as well as ornamental: an iron lantern would be pierced with a fretwork pattern, or candle sconces embossed and crimped, to reflect more light.

Wirework Hook Rack

Using traditional wirework motifs and modern plastic-coated wire, this simple hook rack exemplifies a basic principle of folk art: using everyday materials to create decorative yet practical objects.

YOU WILL NEED
- *green garden wire*
- *broomstick*
- *ruler*
- *wire cutters*
- *pencil*
- *wooden spoon*
- *round-nosed pliers*
- *3 screws*
- *screwdriver*

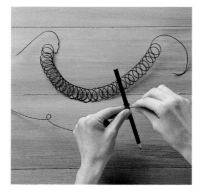

1 Wrap the wire tightly around a broom handle 40 times, leaving a 10cm/4in straight length at each end, and cut off. Flatten the coil between your thumb and fingers. Cut a 56cm/22in length of wire. Form a single loop at the centre and 15cm/6in from each end, by wrapping the wire around a pencil.

2 Thread the looped wire through the flattened coil and slot the wire at each end of the coil through the end loops. The central loop is suspended in the flattened coil. Bend the 15cm/6in section at each end of the wire around a wooden spoon handle to create clover leaves. Use the straight ends of the coiled wire to bind the stems in place.

3 Cut four 30cm/12in lengths of wire. Wrap the centre of each around the spoon handle to make circles. Twist to close. Bend small hooks in the wire ends. Bend each loop in half to make large hooks and hook the ends around the coil and looped wire, closing them tightly.

4 For the centre hook, cut a 2m/79in length of wire. Bend in half and make a small loop. Hold it 15cm/6in from the loop. Twist the wires together. Form a clover leaf with the twisted wire. Bind closed. Slot the hook shank through the coil to lie around the centre loop in the bottom wire. Bend the hook. Screw in place through the loops.

Wire Rolling Pin Holder

This clever device will give a rolling pin a place of its own on the kitchen wall, decorative as well as out of the way. Bend the wire into smooth curves rather than sharp angles.

YOU WILL NEED
- *2mm/¹⁄₁₀in galvanized wire, or two wire coathangers*
- *wire cutters*
- *screwdriver*
- *general-purpose pliers*
- *fine brass picture-hanging wire*

1 Cut two 75cm/30in lengths of wire. Bend the middle of the first length around a screwdriver handle to make a hanging loop. Turn the screwdriver six times.

2 Use the pliers to curl the ends of the wire forwards to make large hooks, and check that the distance between the hooks fits the length of your rolling pin.

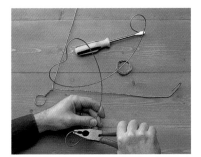

3 Bend the second length of wire sharply in the middle, then bring the ends down in opposite directions to cross over and form a heart shape. Curl the ends. Use short lengths of brass wire to bind the two pieces firmly and neatly together at the points shown.

Fluted Sconce

Two small patisserie moulds find a new and alternative use in this charming sconce, whose rippled surfaces reflect and intensify the soft candlelight beautifully.

You will need
- *protective gloves*
- *tin shears (snips)*
- *30 gauge/¹⁄₁₀₀in tin plate*
- *scalloped madeleine mould*
- *file*
- *wooden block*
- *general-purpose pliers*
- *drill*
- *pop riveter and rivets*
- *oval patisserie mould*
- *permanent marker pen*
- *bradawl (awl)*
- *fine wire*
- *wire cutters*
- *round-nosed pliers*

1 Cut a 20cm/8in strip of tin about 6mm/¼in wider than the base of the scalloped mould. File the edges and corners smooth and drill two holes in one end. Bend back the lip of the mould using pliers and drill two matching holes. Pop rivet the two pieces together.

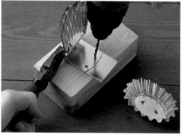

2 Using pliers, bend the tin strip into a right angle to make a shelf. Drill two holes in the base of the oval mould. Place on the shelf and mark the positions of the holes and edge. Drill holes in the shelf. Trim, then file the excess tin. Rivet the mould in place.

3 For the hanger, pierce two holes in the back of the scalloped mould and file. Coil one end of a length of fine wire with round-nose pliers. Pass the uncoiled end from front to back and out of the other hole. Make a second coil and trim.

Twisted Heart Spice Rack

This pretty and ornate wire rack can hang on the wall or stand on a shelf in the kitchen to hold small jars of herbs and spices. Try some of the simpler projects first before attempting this design.

YOU WILL NEED
- *1.65mm/⅛in and*
  0.65mm/¼₀in galvanized wire
- *ruler*
- *wire cutters*
- *permanent marker pen*
- *round-nosed pliers*
- *general-purpose pliers*
- *fine galvanized wire*
- *broom handle*

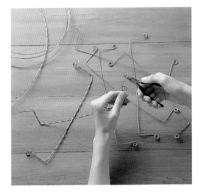

1 Cut five 45cm/18in lengths of the thicker wire. Mark each length 5cm/2in and 10cm/4in in from each end. Using round-nosed pliers, coil the first 5cm/2in of each end, then bend the wire at right angles at the second marked point. Double and twist 8m/26ft of wire. From it cut two 45cm/18in lengths. Mark in the same way. Unravel the first 5cm/2in and make two coils at each end, then bend as before.

2 To make the box section of the rack, cut two 9cm/3½in lengths of twisted wire and join the two struts by twisting the ends of the short wires around them at the bent corners to leave a distance of 6cm/2½in between the struts.

3 Cut a 101cm/40in length of twisted wire and mark it at intervals of 20cm/8in, 12cm/5in, 6cm/2½in, 25cm/10in, 6cm/2½in, 12cm/5in and 20cm/8in. Bend a right angle at each mark to form a rectangular rim. Bend the 20cm/8in section at each end to form the two halves of the heart. Attach the rim to the top of the box using fine wire.

4 Cut four 54cm/21½in lengths of twisted wire. Mark each at intervals of 5cm/2in, 5cm/2in, 6cm/2½in and 38cm/15in. Unravel the first 5cm/2in and bend into two coils. Bend each wire at right angles at the next two points. Coil the long ends then curve two of the wires so they will rest on the back.

5 Slot the box section inside the four coils and tack with fine wire where the pieces touch. Space the plain wire struts made in step 1 evenly across the width of the box and tack in place.

6 Wrap a length of wire around a broom handle to make a loose coil. Position it inside the front of the rack. Using the finer galvanized wire, bind around the rim of the box, securing each piece in position and removing the temporary fixings as you go. Bind from front to back along the bottom struts and bind the decorative spirals where they touch.

Punched Tin Tree Decorations

These embossed decorations are inspired by the folk motifs of eastern Europe. Stamped and die-cut metal artefacts were popular in the nineteenth century, when a tinworker was prominent in every village.

YOU WILL NEED
- *paper for templates*
- *pencil*
- *scissors*
- *36 gauge/¹⁄₂₀₀in aluminium foil*
- *sharp pencil*
- *small, sharp-pointed scissors*
- *permanent marker pen*
- *ruler*
- *cardboard*
- *dressmaker's wheel*
- *ballpoint pen*
- *bradawl (awl)*
- *fine galvanized wire*

1 Copy the templates from the back of the book and cut out. Place the template on a small sheet of aluminium foil and draw around the outline using a sharp pencil. Cut out with sharp-pointed scissors.

2 Mark the main design lines on the back of the decoration using a marker and ruler. Place the decoration face down on cardboard. Trace over the lines using a dress-maker's wheel to emboss the foil.

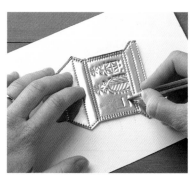

3 Using the picture as a guide, emboss the other details of the decoration with a ballpoint pen. Press firmly to transfer the design.

4 Turn the decoration over and make a hole in the top using a bradawl (awl). Tie a length of fine wire through the hole for hanging.

Needlework

TEXTILES OF ALL KINDS are an essential part of life, and in pre-industrial communities every stitch of clothing and household linen had to be sewn at home, invariably by women, so girls were taught to sew at an early age to help in the never-ending task. They learned not only plain sewing, for making clothes, but more decorative and refined forms of stitchery, including cross stitch, needlepoint and embroidery, and every little girl showed off her skills with a sampler. In remote communities, such as those of early American settlers, every scrap of fabric was carefully recycled, resulting in a rich heritage of patchwork quilts and rag rugs.

Traditional Cross-stitch Sampler

With its soft, faded colouring and traditional style, this sampler could pass for an antique. Add your initials and the present date for a personal touch. The finished stitched area is 23.5 x 28.5cm/9¼ x 11¼in.

You will need
- *50cm/20in square of 32-count raw linen*
- *tacking (basting) thread and needle*
- *masking tape*
- *embroidery frame and tapestry needle*
- *stranded embroidery thread (floss), 1 skein of each colour: yellow, sage, green, khaki, aqua, spruce, teal, blue, rose, coral, wine, umber, dark brown, cream*
- *iron, ironing board and pins*
- *mounting board and picture frame*
- *scalpel*
- *heavyweight non-woven interlining*
- *double-sided adhesive tape*
- *strong thread, scissors*

1 Fold the linen in half in both directions and tack (baste) guide-lines along the folds.

2 Bind the edges with masking tape and place the fabric in the embroidery frame.

3 Starting in the centre and using two strands of cotton (floss) over two threads, work the design from the chart at the back of the book.

4 Remove the embroidery frame and masking tape, pin the design to the ironing board and press.

5 Cut the mounting board to fit the picture frame loosely. Cut the interlining to the same size. Stick the interlining to the board using lengths of double-sided adhesive tape.

6 Place the sampler on the padded board and fold the edges of the linen to the back. Pin opposite sides, pushing the pins into the board.

7 Use strong thread to lace together opposite edges of the linen. Ensure the design is centred on the right side.

8 Make neat, flat folds at the corners, then pin and lace the two remaining edges in the same way. Fit the sampler into the frame.

A Country Angel

This endearing character in her homespun clothes and tightly knotted hair is bound to remain a friend for many years to come.

YOU WILL NEED
- *40 x 25cm/16 x 10in natural calico*
- *40 x 28cm/16 x 11in check cotton – homespun or small-scale gingham*
- *30 x 23cm/12 x 9in blue and white ticking*
- *tea*
- *pencil and paper for templates*
- *scissors*
- *sewing machine*
- *matching thread*
- *polyester wadding (batting)*
- *twigs*
- *secateurs (pruning shears)*
- *fine permanent marker*
- *stranded embroidery cotton (floss) in brown*
- *needle*
- *scrap of red woollen fabric or felt*
- *natural garden twine (jute)*
- *fabric stiffener*
- *copper wire and wire cutters*
- *all-purpose glue*

1 Wash all the fabrics to remove any dressing. While they are damp soak them in tea to give an aged appearance. Trace the patterns from the back of the book. Cut the head and torso out of doubled calico, adding a 1cm/½in seam.

2 Stitch the body pieces together leaving the lower edge open. Clip the curves and turn right side out. Fill with wadding (batting). For legs, cut two twigs 20cm/8in long and place in the body. Sew up the opening, securing the twigs in place.

3 Using the marker, draw the eyes, nose and mouth on to the face. Make French knots with embroidery cotton (floss) around the top of the face for the hair.

4 Cut out the dress. Sew the sides, leaving the sleeves and hem raw. Cut a slit for the neck and turn through. Cut a red wool heart and attach with a cross stitch. Dress the angel. Place short twigs in the sleeves. Secure with twine (jute).

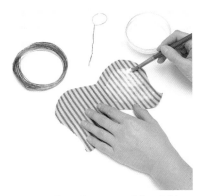

5 Cut the wings out of the ticking and fray the raw edges slightly. Apply fabric stiffener liberally to the wings to soak them thoroughly. Lay them flat to dry. Make a halo from copper wire, leaving a long end to glue to the wings.

6 Stitch the wings securely to the back of the body through the dress. Attach the halo.

Hands and Hearts Throw

Use your own hand as the template for this traditional quilted throw. The symbolic motifs and check cotton fabrics are typical of American folk designs, lending a homespun quality to the throw. As well as being decorative, the buttons serve to quilt the layers together.

YOU WILL NEED
- *pencil*
- *paper for template*
- *pen*
- *scissors*
- *fusible bonding web*
- *iron*
- *scraps of check cotton fabrics*
- *1.5m/60in square of heavy cream cotton fabric*
- *dressmaker's pins*
- *sewing machine*
- *matching threads*
- *1.6m/64in square of check cotton backing fabric*
- *1.5m/60in square of polyester wadding (batting)*
- *safety pins*
- *stranded embroidery thread (floss)*
- *needle*
- *assorted buttons*

1 To make the templates, trace your hand on a sheet of paper. Re-draw the shape, simplifying it, and cut out. Draw and cut out a heart of an appropriate size.

2 Trace the hand template on the paper backing of the fusible bonding web. Cut out roughly. Iron the bonding web on to the wrong side of a piece of check fabric and cut accurately around the outline.

3 Transfer the heart to the web in the same way. Iron it to the wrong side of a contrasting piece of fabric. Cut out. Remove the paper backing, then bond on to the hand.

4 Make 11 more hands, varying the fabrics, and attach a heart to each in the same way. Peel off the backing paper from the hands.

▶

5 Place the cream fabric on a clean, flat surface. Position the hands randomly, leaving a border of about 25cm/10in around the edge of the throw. Pin, then iron in place.

6 Using matching threads, machine stitch around both the hand and heart shapes in a close zig-zag stitch.

7 Place the backing fabric right side down. Centre the wadding (batting) on top. Place the appliqué on top, right side up. Working from the centre outwards, secure the three layers together with safety pins. Trim the wadding (batting) if necessary so that the backing fabric is 6cm/2½in larger all around.

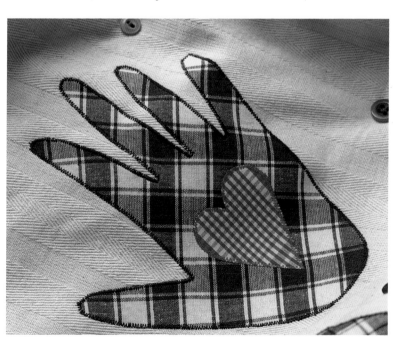

Above: Detail showing the closely worked satin stitch covering the raw edges.

8 Turn in a 1cm/½in double hem of the backing over to the right side of the throw to make a 5cm/2in border. Press. Pin, then stitch, mitring the corners. Using six strands of embroidery thread (floss), sew buttons between the hand shapes.

Patchwork Cushion Cover

The pattern for this cushion comes from a single block of a very large sampler quilt made in Pennsylvania in about 1870, and this adaptation uses the original colours of the quilt. Use closely woven cotton fabrics, as they stay in shape and do not fray much. The finished cushion is 40cm/16in square.

YOU WILL NEED
- *graph paper or access to a photocopier*
- *pencil*
- *template plastic*
- *ruler*
- *25cm/10in red fabric 120cm/ 48in wide*
- *25cm/10in green fabric 120cm/48in wide*
- *45cm/18in yellow fabric 120cm/48in wide*
- *scraps of bright green and red spotted fabrics*
- *scissors*
- *dressmaker's pins*
- *sewing machine*
- *matching threads*
- *iron*
- *needle*
- *cushion pad*

PATCHES
Red: 20 of no. 1;
6 of no. 4; 2 of no. 9;
4 of no. 10
Green: 8 of no. 5;
4 of no. 11; 2 of no. 6;
5 of no. 12; 4 of no. 13
Yellow: 5 of no. 2; 6 of no. 3;
8 of no. 5; 4 of no. 7
Bright green: 4 of no. 8
Red spotted: 4 of no. 11

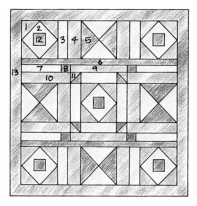

1 Enlarge the design to the finished size of the cushion. Number the templates as shown, then trace them on to template plastic, adding a 6mm/¼in seam allowance on all sides. Use the templates to cut out the shapes list-ed, laying out the whole block to check that you have all the pieces.

2 Join the pieces working in rows. For the corners and centre block, with right sides together, pin and sew two red triangles to opposite sides of a yellow square. Press, with the seam allowance under the darker fabric. Join the two remaining red triangles to the other two sides. Press flat.

3 For the remaining four blocks, pin and stitch one yellow triangle to one green triangle. Repeat with two more triangles. Join the two pieces diagonally, aligning seams to make a square and press.

4 Stitch the yellow and red vertical sashing together, then join all the pieces to make the top row. Press. Press under a 6mm/¼in hem all around the green squares and appliqué them by hand, using yellow thread and tiny stitches.

5 Piece the other rows in the same way using the pattern as a guide, then join them together, pressing between each step, until the cushion front is complete.

6 Pin two of the green border pieces to opposite sides of the cushion front. Stitch and press, then repeat on the remaining sides.

7 For the cushion back, cut a piece of yellow the same width as the front and 12.5cm/5in longer. Cut in half. Stitch a double hem along one long end of each piece. Place the cushion front and backs right sides together, hemmed edges overlapping. Pin and stitch. Clip the corners and turn through.

Coiled Rag Rug

Plaiting, or braiding, is one of the simplest techniques for making rag rugs, and needs no special equipment. Change the colours as you work, alternating light and dark fabrics.

YOU WILL NEED
- ♦ *at least 8 assorted fabrics of similar weight, such as printed cotton dress fabrics*
- ♦ *scissors*
- ♦ *dressmaker's pins*
- ♦ *needle*
- ♦ *matching thread*
- ♦ *safety pin*
- ♦ *metal cuphook*
- ♦ *80cm/32in square backing fabric*

1 Cut or tear the fabrics into 5cm/2in strips. Hand stitch the strips end to end, with right sides together. Make three strips, each measuring about 100cm/40in.

2 Fasten the ends of the three strips together with a safety pin. Hook the pin over a cuphook screwed securely into a flat surface just above eye level.

3 To plait (braid) the strips, bring the right-hand strip over the middle strip, then the left-hand strip over the new middle strip. Continue, turning the raw edges in as much as possible, until about 20cm/8in of each strip remains. Secure the loose ends with a pin. Remove the safety pin and taper the beginning of the plait (braid) by trimming the fabric strips. Stitch neatly to conceal the raw edges.

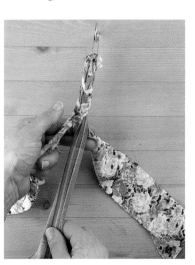

4 Coil the plait around the tapered end and stitch invisibly. Keep the work flat without pulling the thread tight. Every so often, pass the needle right through the plait to secure it to the coil.

5 When you reach the end, add more strips of fabric and plait them. In this way you can change the colours as the rug grows. When the rug reaches a diameter of 75cm/30in, taper the strips. Stitch the end neatly against the rug.

6 Place the rug on the backing fabric and cut around it leaving a turning allowance of 2cm/¾in. Place the rug right side down and pin the backing fabric to it, turning in the allowance. Back stitch across the backing fabric, working from the centre outwards in an asterisk pattern. Hem stitch around the edge of the rug.

Woodwork

❤

By its nature, folk art developed among people who were not wealthy and did not have access to exotic or expensive materials. The tradition of painting or graining wooden furniture arose because furniture had to be made from pine, rather than fine-grained hardwoods that would have needed no further embellishment. Woodcarving often combined ornament with function, as in the case of carved butter-moulds which served to identify a particular farmer's produce. Small objects, such as spoons and toys, might be carved to help while away long hours tending sheep or cattle. Woodburning, which could withstand vigorous scrubbing, was used to decorate kitchen utensils.

Painted Checkerboard

This board follows the pattern of old draughtboards or checkerboards, which were often made by sign painters and came in a variety of decorative designs. They always included divisions for the players' winnings. The stars and stripes are a popular folk pattern and were the design source for the decoration on this checkerboard.

YOU WILL NEED
- *6mm/¼in plywood,*
  30 x 45cm/12 x 18in
- *2.5 x 1cm/1 x ½in pine strip,*
  1.7m/5ft 6in long
- *saw*
- *wood glue*
- *panel pins (brads)*
- *hammer*
- *ruler*
- *pencil*
- *60cm/24in narrow pine strip*
- *household paintbrush and*
  artist's fine-pointed brush
- *matt emulsion (flat latex) paint:*
  pumpkin yellow, off-white and
  brick red
- *artist's acrylic paint: jade green,*
  cobalt blue and burnt umber
- *cloth*
- *five-pointed star stamp cut*
  from foam
- *acrylic matt (flat) varnish*

1 To make the board, saw four lengths of pine strip to fit the four sides of the plywood.

2 Mitre the corners to fit neatly. Glue and nail in place with panel pins (brads). Allow to dry.

3 Measure and mark out the central square for the playing surface and glue and pin the two edging strips in place.

4 Paint the base, sides and dividing strips pumpkin yellow, the rectangular end sections jade green and the central square off-white.

5 Paint brick red over the pumpkin yellow, then rub it off with a cloth while it is still wet.

6 Draw up a grid by dividing the sides into eight equal parts. Carefully fill in alternate squares using brick red and an artist's brush.

7 Brush on a thinned coat of cobalt blue and then wipe it back while still wet. Using off-white paint and a star stamp, print across the blue end sections. Blot excess paint from the stamp before printing.

8 Give the whole board a coat of varnish tinted with burnt umber, working it well into the corners to give them a slightly darker tone.

Colonial-style Birdhouse

Folk art techniques inspired the subtle colouring and distressed paint finish on this little nesting-box.
It makes a desirable springtime retreat to attract small birds to your garden.

YOU WILL NEED
- *6mm/¼in medium density fibre-board (MDF) or exterior-grade plywood*
- *small piece of timber for base*
- *pencil and ruler*
- *saw*
- *protective face mask*
- *drill*
- *padsaw or coping saw*
- *medium-grade sandpaper*
- *wood glue*
- *hammer*
- *panel pins (brads)*
- *matt emulsion (flat latex) paint: blue-grey and white*
- *paintbrush*
- *lead or copper sheet*
- *tin shears (snips)*
- *staple gun and staples*
- *copper wire*
- *wire cutters*

1 Enlarge the template provided. Draw the house on MDF and cut out. Drill a starter hole in the box front and cut out the entrance using a padsaw. Sand the edges. Assemble the walls and base using wood glue and panel pins (brads). Attach only the shorter roof piece.

3 Cut a strip of lead or copper the depth of the roof and 5cm/2in wide. Staple this to the loose roof piece.

4 Position on the house, bend the lead to fit and staple through the lead into the fixed roof half.

2 Paint the house and roof blue-grey. When dry, paint the house walls white. Leave to dry then rub back with sandpaper to reveal some of the base coat.

5 Drill two holes just below and to each side of the entrance. Bend a length of wire into a flattened loop slightly wider than the distance between the holes. Pass the two ends of the wire through the holes and turn them down inside the box to hold the perch in place.

Bridal Chest

One item of furniture common to almost all folk art culture is the dower or bridal chest, designed to hold all the needlework and linen the bride spent her girlhood preparing.

YOU WILL NEED
- *old or new pine chest, preferably with feet (the one shown measures 94 x 46 x 32cm/37 x 18 x 13in)*
- *matt emulsion (flat latex) paint: brick red, dark reddish brown and creamy yellow*
- *household paintbrushes and artist's brushes*
- *cloth*
- *paper for template*
- *transfer paper*
- *soft and sharp pencils*
- *long ruler or straight edge*
- *masking tape*
- *artist's acrylic paint: reddish brown, red, brown, blue-green, yellow ochre, raw umber*
- *wooden batten (straight edge) mounted on blocks*
- *acrylic matt (flat) varnish*

1 Prepare then paint the chest surface with brick red (latex) paint.

2 Thin the reddish brown emulsion with an equal amount of water. Apply liberally over the dry base coat.

3 Use the brush vigorously, changing direction often, aiming for an uneven texture. Wipe some of the paint off with a cloth to simulate an old and worn appearance.

4 Enlarge the template to fit the front panels of the chest. Position as desired. Place a sheet of transfer paper between the template and chest and trace the outline.

5 Repeat, using a straight edge to ensure that the baselines match. Fill in the background of each panel using creamy yellow emulsion paint. Leave to dry.

6 With the chest on its back, re-position the pattern and transfer paper over each painted panel. Secure with masking tape. Carefully trace the whole pattern on to the panel.

7 Practise brushstrokes until your wrist has loosened up, then work around the border using reddish brown acrylic paint thinned with water. Support your wrist and keep the strokes flowing and not stiff.

8 Thin the red acrylic paint with water and add the fine curved strokes to the border using a fine-pointed brush. Use the same brush with thinned brown acrylic to paint the leaves and stems in the centre.

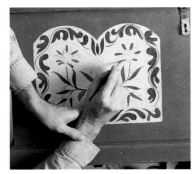

9 Paint alternate flower petals and lower leaves using thinned blue-green acrylic.

10 Complete the flowers, filling in the red petals and the yellow ochre lower leaves. Check the pattern to make sure you have painted all the elements.

11 Outline the inner panel using a fine brush and reddish brown paint. Use the raised straight edge to guide your brush. You may need to thin the paint further to get a smooth line. If you make a mistake, let the paint dry then paint carefully over with the background colour.

▶

12 Position your choice of motif on top of the chest using the same method as for the panels: trace them down then paint alternate sections in brown and brick red emulsion (latex) paint.

13 Mark a square border around each motif using a pencil; align it with the front panel. Using the raised batten (straight edge) as a guide, paint the border in thinned brown acrylic paint with an artist's 2.5cm/1in square-tipped brush.

14 Tint some clear acrylic varnish with a little raw umber acrylic paint and apply two even coats to the whole chest. Allow the varnish to dry thoroughly between coats. Finish with one coat of untinted varnish.

Painted Sheep Sign

Painted signs were a common sight outside shops and taverns in eighteenth-century towns. Recognizable symbols, such as the tailor's scissors or butcher's pig, were designed to guide even the illiterate customer in the right direction. This sheep sign can be hung on the wall from hooks, or you can attach a mitre-cut plank at the back to act as a stand.

You will need
- *pencil and paper for template*
- *6mm/¼in plywood, 90 x 60cm/ 36 x 24in*
- *coping saw or jigsaw*
- *medium and coarse-grade sandpaper*
- *matt emulsion (flat latex) paint in off-white*
- *household paintbrushes, stencilling brush and artist's fine-pointed brush*
- *artist's acrylic paints: deep grass green, black, burnt umber, raw umber and raw sienna*
- *acrylic matt (flat) varnish*

1 Enlarge the pattern provided and transfer the outline of the sheep design to the plywood. Cut out and sand the sawn edges.

2 Paint the sheep white, using random "scruffy" brushstrokes in all directions. Paint the grass and black legs.

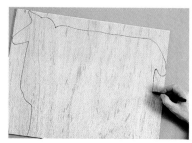

3 Mix burnt umber into the off-white paint to obtain two shades of beige, and apply these with the stencil brush. Use the darker shade around the edges and under the chin first, and gradually build up the colour and texture of a fleece. Add highlights to the legs in dark beige.

4 Rub back the paint in patches to reveal the base coat and add highlights, without losing the woolly texture. Paint an eye and a happy mouth with a fine brush. Apply a coat of varnish tinted with a little raw umber and raw sienna, followed by a coat of clear varnish.

Decoy Birds

Wooden birds were originally made for the practical purpose of deceiving real birds into flying within range of the hunter's gun. These stylized little birds are sawn from an old plank, and the rustic effect is enhanced by mounting them on a base made of rough weathered wood.

YOU WILL NEED

- *paper for templates*
- *pencil*
- *scissors*
- *felt-tipped pen*
- *piece of floorboard or other reclaimed timber*
- *clamp*
- *drill*
- *padsaw or coping saw*
- *hacksaw*
- *1m/38in length of 7mm/⅜in dowelling (dowel)*
- *piece of driftwood or rough weathered wood*
- *artist's acrylic paints: red, yellow, dark green, dark brown, white and black*
- *medium and fine paintbrushes*
- *fine-grade sandpaper*
- *white glue*
- *acrylic matt (flat) varnish (optional)*

1 Enlarge and cut out the templates provided. Using a felt-tipped pen, draw around each bird directly on to the floorboard or reclaimed timber.

2 Clamp the board to a firm surface. Drill a small starter hole outside the edge of the first shape, then saw around the marked line. Repeat for the other birds.

3 Cut the dowelling (dowel) into three 20cm/8in and two 18cm/7in pieces.

4 Drill a 7mm/⅜in hole in the centre bottom of each bird and five holes in the driftwood base, spacing them so that the birds will sit comfortably.

5 Paint each bird in a different colour and add beaks and eyes in black. Leave to dry then sand down to reveal the wood along the edges of each bird.

6 Glue the dowel into the base, then glue the birds on top to make an attractive group. If desired, apply a coat of varnish.

Nature's Store

THE LIFE of small, rural communities was punctuated by
seasonal celebrations that reflected the natural cycle, since it
was this that dominated their fortunes and could mean the
difference between feast or famine, life or death. For
centuries, traditional decorations made from natural materials
have been associated with occasions such as Easter, Harvest
and Hallowe'en. Folk artists looked for their raw materials in
and around their homes, and nature's bounty was an
important source for them, as well as inspiring many of their
favourite and most commonly used motifs, such as fruit,
flowers, birds and animals.

Heart-carved Pumpkin

The heart motif is common to many cultures and symbolizes divine as well as human love. This glowing pumpkin lantern has been carved with a generous heart in a traditional central European style.

YOU WILL NEED
- *water-soluble crayon*
- *pumpkin*
- *kitchen knife*
- *ice cream scoop*
- *craft knife*
- *paper for template*
- *dressmaker's pins*
- *large needle*
- *lino-cutting tool*

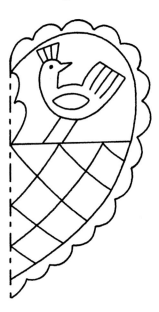

1 Using the crayon, draw a circle on the top of the pumpkin. Cut around it with the kitchen knife. Scoop out the seeds and flesh using the ice cream scoop, leaving a shell 1cm/½in thick. Draw a scalloped edge around the opening and cut it away using the craft knife.

2 Copy the template below left, enlarging it as required. Secure the template to the front of the pumpkin using dressmaker's pins. Use a large needle to prick along all the lines of the design.

3 Carve out the design using a lino-cutting tool, following the pin-pricked lines.

4 Draw freehand branches to each side of the heart to create a frame. Use the lino-cutting tool to carve the leaves.

Paper-cut Eggs

The folk craft of paper-cutting has a long tradition in Switzerland, where very intricate symmetrical designs are cut from folded black paper, usually depicting the natural world and village life. This beautiful craft is easily adapted to curved surfaces, as the intricate shapes make the paper-cut very flexible.

YOU WILL NEED
- *sharp-pointed scissors*
- *black craft paper*
- *pinking shears*
- *blown white hens' eggs*
- *ready-mixed wallpaper paste (fungicide-free)*
- *paintbrush*
- *tracing paper and pencil*
- *paper clips*
- *acrylic matt (flat) varnish*

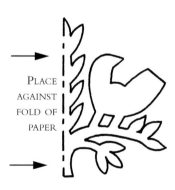

PLACE
AGAINST
FOLD OF
PAPER

1 Cut a straight strip of paper 2mm/⅛in wide. Using pinking shears, cut two strips 2mm/⅛in wide. All three strips should be long enough to fit lengthways around an egg.

2 Smear some wallpaper paste lengthways around the middle of the egg and on the paper strips. Stick the strips around the egg using the photograph as a guide.

3 Trace the template provided on the left of the page. Fold a small piece of black paper in half and place the straight side of the template against the fold. Secure it with a paper clip, cut around the design and remove the template.

4 Smear wallpaper paste on the side of the egg and on the back of the cut-out. Place it centrally on the egg and smooth out carefully. Repeat on the other side. Leave to dry before coating the egg with acrylic varnish.

Heart of Wheat

Fashion a heart at harvest time, when wheat is plentiful, for a delightful decoration that will look good adorning a wall or a dresser at any time of the year. Despite its delicate feathery looks, this heart is quite robust and should last many years.

You will need
- *scissors*
- *heavy-duty garden wire*
- *florist's tape*
- *florist's wire*
- *large bunch of wheat*

1 Cut three long lengths of heavy-gauge wire and bend them into a heart shape. Twist the ends together at the bottom. Use florist's tape to bind the wire heart.

2 Using florist's wire, make up enough small bundles of wheat ears to densely cover the wire heart. Leave a short length of wire at each end for fixing to the heart.

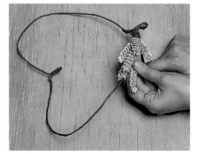

3 Starting at the bottom of the wire shape, tape the first bundle of wheat ears to the heart.

4 Place the second bundle further up the heart behind the first, and tape it in position. Continue until the whole heart is covered.

5 For the bottom, wire together about six bunches of wheat ears, twist the wires together and fasten them to the heart, finishing off with florist's tape to neaten.

Shaker-style Spice Wreath

This flexible wreath is inspired by the herbal gifts made in Shaker communities. The same idea can be adapted to make a garland, perhaps to decorate a table: just continue threading the various elements until you have the length you need.

YOU WILL NEED
- *picture framer's gilt (gilder's) wax*
- *dried oranges*
- *natural raffia*
- *cinnamon sticks*
- *large-eyed needle*
- *dried bay leaves*

1 Rub picture framer's gilt (gilder's) wax on to the oranges. Wind a strand of raffia several times around a bundle of three cinnamon sticks, then tie up the bundle, leaving the ends of the raffia in place. Thread another strand of raffia under the tie, at the opposite side to the knot. Pull through until its ends are even, then knot securely.

2 Thread both ends of the raffia strand into the needle and then thread on about 20 bay leaves, an orange, then 20 more leaves. Unthread the needle and wind the raffia twice around a second bundle of three cinnamon sticks. Tie to secure in place.

3 Re-thread the needle and repeat the sequence until the garland is 85cm/34in long. To complete the wreath, using a reef knot, tie the end of the raffia to the long ends left at the beginning. Trim the ends.

Appliquéd Scented Sachet

Use this pretty lavender sachet to scent a drawer: if you keep the design simple, it won't take long to make a whole batch. You can make them up from different fabric scraps or, as here, use the same fabric but create interest by reversing it or cutting it on the cross for the appliquéd decoration.

YOU WILL NEED
- *2 pieces of fabric, 10cm/4in square*
- *a heart shape cut from the same fabric, 5cm/2in high*
- *stranded embroidery thread (floss)*
- *needle*
- *coloured shell button*
- *dressmaker's pins*
- *sewing machine*
- *matching thread*
- *scissors*
- *dried lavender*
- *50cm/20in length of 1cm/½in grosgrain ribbon*

1 Place the heart right side up on the centre front of one fabric square. Using blanket stitch or any decorative embroidery stitch and stranded embroidery thread (floss), sew the heart in place.

2 Stitch a contrasting button just below the dip in the top of the heart. Pin the second fabric square right side down on the appliquéd square.

3 Machine stitch the two squares together, leaving a small opening. Snip off the corners and turn to the right side. Fill with lavender and slip-stitch the opening.

4 Fold the grosgrain ribbon over the edges of the lavender sachet and slip-stitch in position on both sides, folding in the corners neatly.

Templates

Enlarge the templates to the required size using a photocopier. Alternatively, place a grid over the page and on another larger grid, chart the points where each design line crosses the grid. Join up the marked points to create the outline.

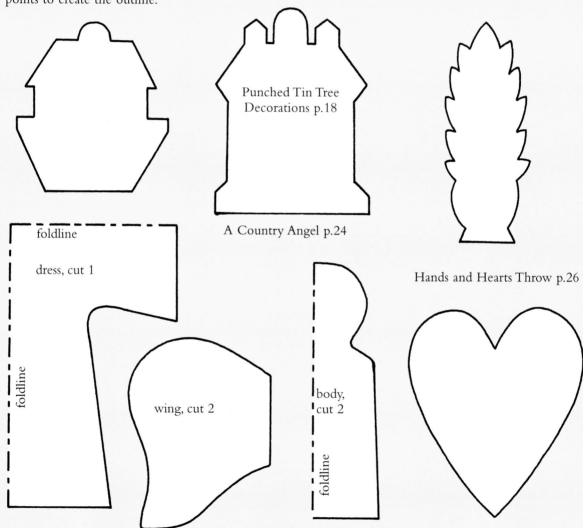

Punched Tin Tree
Decorations p.18

A Country Angel p.24

Hands and Hearts Throw p.26

foldline

dress, cut 1

foldline

wing, cut 2

body,
cut 2

foldline

Colonial-style Birdhouse p.38

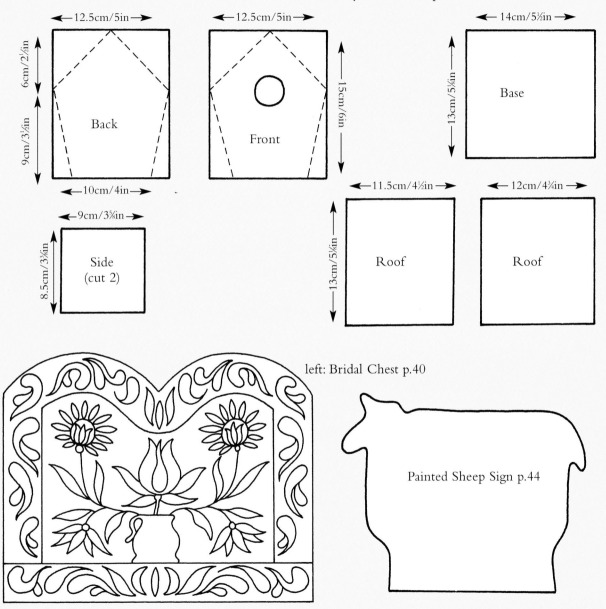

←— 12.5cm/5in —→

6cm/2½in

9cm/3½in

Back

←— 10cm/4in —→

←— 12.5cm/5in —→

15cm/6in

Front

←— 14cm/5½in —→

13cm/5⅛in

Base

←9cm/3⅝in→

8.5cm/3⅜in

Side
(cut 2)

←— 11.5cm/4½in —→

13cm/5⅛in

Roof

←— 12cm/4¾in —→

Roof

left: Bridal Chest p.40

Painted Sheep Sign p.44

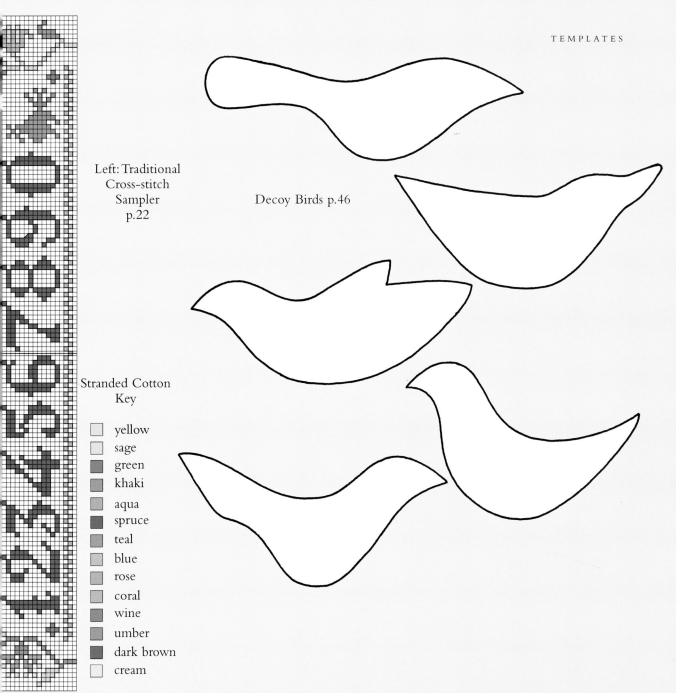

Left: Traditional
Cross-stitch
Sampler
p.22

Decoy Birds p.46

Stranded Cotton
Key

- yellow
- sage
- green
- khaki
- aqua
- spruce
- teal
- blue
- rose
- coral
- wine
- umber
- dark brown
- cream

Index

angel, country, 24–5
appliquéd scented sachet, 58–9

bay leaves, Shaker-style spice wreath, 56–7
birdhouse, colonial-style, 38–9
birds, decoy, 46–7
bridal chest, 40–3

checkerboard, painted, 36–7
chest, bridal, 40–3
coiled rag rug, 32–3
colonial-style birdhouse, 38–9
country angel, 24–5
cross -stitch sampler, traditional 22–3
cushion cover, patchwork, 29–31

decoy birds, 46–7

eggs, paper-cut, 52–3
embroidery, traditional cross-stitch sampler, 22–3

fabric projects, 20–33
    appliquéd scented sachet, 58–9
    coiled rag rug, 32–3
    country angel, 24–5
    hand and hearts throw, 26–8
    patchwork cushion cover, 29–31
    traditional cross-stitch sampler, 22–3
fluted sconce, 15

hand and hearts throw, 26–8
    hook rack, wirework, 12–13

lavender, appliquéd scented sachet, 58–9

metalworking projects, 10–19
    fluted sconce, 15
    punched tin tree decorations, 18–19
    twisted heart spice rack, 16–17
    wire rolling pin holder, 14
    wirework hook rack, 12–13

nature's store projects
    appliquéd scented sachet, 58–9
    heart-carved pumpkin, 50–1
    paper-cut eggs, 52–3
    Shaker-style spice wreath, 56–7
    wheat, heart of, 54–5

oranges, Shaker-style spice wreath, 56–7

painted projects:
    bridal chest, 40–3
    decoy birds, 46–7
    painted checkerboard, 36–7
    painted sheep sign, 44–5
paper-cut eggs, 52–3
patchwork cushion cover, 29–31
plaiting (braiding), coiled rag rug, 32-3
pumpkin, heart-carved, 50–1
punched tin tree decorations, 18–19

racks:
    twisted heart spice rack, 16–17
    wirework hook rack, 12–13
rag rug, coiled 32–3
rolling pin holder, 14
rug, coiled rag, 32–3

sampler, traditional cross-stitch, 22–3
scented sachet, appliquéd, 58–9
sconce, fluted, 15
Shaker-style spice wreath, 56–7
sign, painted sheep, 44–5
spice rack, twisted heart, 16–17
spice wreath, Shaker-style, 56–7

templates, 60–3
throw, hand and hearts, 26–8
traditional cross-stitch sampler, 22–3
tree decorations, punched tin, 18–19
twisted heart spice rack, 16–17

wheat, heart of, 54–5
wire rolling pin holder, 14
wirework hook rack, 12–13
wooden projects, 34–47
    bridal chest, 40–3
    colonial-style birdhouse, 38–9
    decoy birds, 46–7
    painted checkerboard, 36–7
    painted sheep sign, 44–5
wreath, Shaker-style, 56–7